Pink, Blue,
& All the SHADES of You!

Pink, Blue, & All the SHADES of You!

Written by
Phoenix Schneider

Illustrated by
Isa Goldfarb

Copyright © 2018 by Phoenix Schneider
All rights reserved. No part of this book may be reproduced in any form
without written permission from the publisher
Illustrations by Isa Goldfarb.
Visit www.coachphoenix.com

Designed by Stephanie Czapla

Dedicated to my niece Destiny, who inspires me every day.
At five years old, she told me she was a boy because she only liked "boy" toys.
When I told her that all toys were for every gender, she said
she was a girl and went back to making her clock with building blocks.
Thank you to my mom, for loving me unconditionally
and encouraging me to make a difference in the world.
For my partner Jessica, thank you for believing in me and for being
my magical soul-unicorn.
- Phoenix -

Dedicated to Pearl Olanoff and Frances Seidman, who both
did so much for the children.
- Isa -

Some kids play with dolls.
Some play with trucks.

This kid races on horses and ducks!

Some kids like blue. Some kids like pink. This kid paints their nails like a bright colored drink!

Some kids have walls
with planets and moons.

This kid has a
kung fu-themed
dinosaur room!

Some kids ride skateboards.
Some kids fly kites.

These kids pop wheelies all day and night!

Some kids play football. Some kids dance ballet.

These kids score touchdowns and **shake shake** their **bootay!**

Some kids play baseball.
Some kids dance hip-hop.

These kids hit homeruns then do twirly bip-bops!

Some kids bake brownies with sprinkles and fudge.

This kid is baking with sugar and love!

Some kids play videos.
Some paint and draw.
These friends are building a house for their dog!

Made in the
USA
Middletown, DE